BTEC FIRST

Business

Student Workbook

Andrew Dean and Louise Stubbs

Published by Collins Education
An imprint of HarperCollins Publishers
77–85 Fulham Palace Road
Hammersmith
London
W6 8JB

Browse the complete Collins Education catalogue at
www.collinseducation.com

© HarperCollins Publishers Limited 2010
10 9 8 7 6 5 4 3 2 1

ISBN 978 0 00 734269 3

Andrew Dean and Louise Stubbs assert the moral right to be identified as the authors of this work.

All rights reserved. No part of this publication may be reproduced, stored in a retrieval system or transmitted in any form or by any means – electronic, mechanical, photocopying, recording or otherwise – without the prior written consent of the Publisher or a licence permitting restricted copying in the United Kingdom issued by the Copyright Licensing Agency Ltd, 90 Tottenham Court Road, London W1T 4LP.

British Library Cataloguing in Publication Data.
A Catalogue record for this publication is available from the British Library.

Commissioned by Emma Woolf
Project managed and edited by Jo Kemp
Design and typesetting by Thomson Digital
Text design by Nigel Jordan
Cover design by Angela English
Picture research by Geoff Holdsworth/Pictureresearch.co.uk
Printed and bound by Martins the Printers, Berwick upon Tweed

Photographic acknowledgements

Fishburn Hedges (2/www.talktofrank.com); iStockphoto (4/lisafx); iStockphoto (11/Lisa F. Young); Alamy (13/D. Hurst); Alamy (15/Kevin Britland); iStockphoto (19/Mark Hatfield); iStockphoto (35/Alexander Raths).

Contents

1	**Understanding the purpose and ownership of business**		1
	1.1 The purpose and ownership of business		2
	1.2 Understanding the context in which businesses operate		6
2	**Business organisations**		9
	2.1 Setting business aims and objectives		10
	2.2 The main functional areas in business organisations		12
3	**Financial forecasting for business**		17
	3.1 Costs, revenues and profits in a business organisation		18
	3.2 Break-even analysis		20
	3.3 Creating a cash flow forecast		24
4	**People in organisations**		29
	4.1 Job roles and functions in organisations		30
	4.2 Producing documentation for specific job roles		32
	4.3 Preparing for employment		35
Glossary			39
Student notes			42

Introduction

This workbook is made up of questions and activities that cover each section of Units 1, 2, 3 and 4 of the BTEC First in Business qualification. The questions and activities are designed to develop and assess your knowledge and understanding of a range of topics that are part of these units. To get the most out of using this workbook as part of your BTEC First in Business studies, you need to understand that:

- What you learn from studying Units 1, 2, 3 and 4 with your class tutors and from using a textbook written for the BTEC First in Business qualification will provide you with the background knowledge needed to complete the questions and activities in this workbook.
- You should complete the questions and activities after you have studied the corresponding part of each unit using textbooks and other resources with your tutor or as your tutor directs.
- It is best to complete the questions and activities for each unit before you begin any of the assessment tasks associated with each unit. Completing the questions and activities to the best of your ability will help to prepare you for these important assessments.
- The mark allocations and the number of answer lines provided for each question or activity are a guide to how much you should write.
- Where a question asks you to provide a specific number of examples ('Give three examples of…') or to identify a specific number of reasons ('Describe two reasons why…'), your answer must provide the specified number of items to achieve full marks. Providing more examples or more reasons than the question requires will not gain you any more marks so it is best not to do this.

When Edexcel set controlled assessment tasks and assignment questions they choose their words very carefully. You need to understand that the way a question is asked or the way a task is worded is very important. Always make sure that you look at, understand and respond to the command verb – for example, 'describe', 'explain' – in order to get the right level of detail in your answer. 'Name' and 'give' are low level question verbs for 1 or 2 marks, 'describe' usually requires more detail for 2 or more marks, 'explain' typically requires more detail again and 'evaluate' requires the most detail.

Finally, when answering questions, make sure that you write clearly and spell correctly. This is very important when using the specialist words and phrases of the business world.

Answers can be found at: www.collinseducation.com/btecbusiness

Unit 1: Understanding the purpose and ownership of business

This unit covers the following topics:
- the purpose and ownership of business
- the business context in which organisations operate.

Your learning in this unit will be assessed through assignments that are set and marked by your tutor in accordance with grading criteria and standards set by Edexcel. The assignments will require you to focus on:
- exploring and evaluating the ownership and purposes of different types of business organisations
- demonstrating that you understand how businesses operate and respond to changes in the business environment.

The questions and activities that follow provide you with an opportunity to develop your knowledge and assess your understanding of the range of topics that are part of Unit 1.

Answers can be found at: www.collinseducation.com/btecbusiness

Topic 1.1 The purpose and ownership of business

1.1 The purpose and ownership of business

A number of different types of business organisations exist in the United Kingdom. They range from multinational companies to small local businesses. While all businesses contribute to the national wellbeing by providing employment and generating income, they also have a wide range of different purposes. The questions and activities that follow provide you with opportunities to develop and show your understanding of:

▶ *the purpose of businesses*, including supply of goods and services, e.g. at a profit, free, at cost, for sale below cost

▶ *ownership of businesses*, e.g. sole trader, partnership, limited companies (private ltd and public plc), charities, voluntary organisations, co-operatives, government

▶ *the size of businesses*, e.g. small, medium, large

▶ *the scale of businesses*, e.g. local, regional, national, European and global organisations

▶ *the classification of businesses*, including primary (e.g. farming, forestry, fishing, extraction/mining), secondary (e.g. manufacturing, engineering, construction), tertiary (e.g. private service industries, local and national public services, voluntary/not-for-profit services).

Questions and activities

1. Businesses seek to provide their customers with the correct product or service to match what they really want.

   Complete the table below to show whether the company given provides a product or a service. **(6 marks)**

Company	Product or service?
Thomas Cook	
HMV	
NHS	
talktofrank.com	
Apple	
Ebay	

2

Unit 1 Understanding the purpose and ownership of business

> Most businesses' main aim is to make a profit. However, some businesses, such as Divine Chocolate, focus on the sustainability of their suppliers and the company itself.

2. List two other reasons why someone might open a business. **(2 marks)**

> It has become more and more important for football clubs in the Premier League to have stable finances. Manchester United and Portsmouth are just two examples of clubs that have struggled with large debt.

3. Arsenal FC has just announced a record profit for the year 2009/2010. What is meant by the term 'profit'? **(2 marks)**

4. Why is it important for businesses to make a profit? **(4 marks)**

> Some supermarkets sell some necessity goods such as eggs, milk and bread at cost price.

5. What is meant by the term 'cost price'? **(1 mark)**

6. Why do you think some supermarkets use this pricing strategy? **(5 marks)**

Topic 1.1 The purpose and ownership of business

Companies like Tesco, Apple and McDonalds are famous examples of private sector businesses, owned by a group of people, aiming to make large profits. The public sector runs slightly differently.

7. What is meant by the 'public sector'? **(2 marks)**

_____
_____
_____
_____

8. Why is it necessary for the public sector to exist? **(4 marks)**

_____
_____
_____
_____

Edward had always wanted to be self-employed plumber, owning his own business. He had dreamed of being his own boss from the age of 15. In January 2010, Edward started his own company, 'Water King'. He has chosen to set this up as a sole trader.

9. Give two characteristics of a business set up as a sole trader. **(2 marks)**

_____
_____

Edward managed to achieve his boyhood dream of being his own boss. However, he couldn't have done this without the funding he received from friends and family.

10. List three other examples of businesses that are normally set up as a sole trader. **(3 marks)**

_____
_____
_____

11. Explain the benefits to Edward of opening 'Water King' as a sole trader. **(5 marks)**

_____
_____
_____
_____
_____

Unit 1 Understanding the purpose and ownership of business

> You may decide that you want to set up your own business. TV programmes like Dragons Den help inspire new entrepreneurs in the UK. However, it is important to choose the correct type of ownership!
>
> After 3 months of working as a sole trader, Edward allowed his friend Ali to come in as a partner. They changed the business from a sole trader to a partnership.

12. In the table below, list a key advantage and a key disadvantage of setting up a business as a sole trader, limited company, partnership and plc. **(8 marks)**

Type of business ownership	Advantage	Disadvantage
Sole trader		
Private limited company (Ltd)		
Partnership		
Public limited company (plc)		

> Public limited companies allow members of the public to buy shares in them. This is a great way to generate capital which the business can use to invest. Tesco has enjoyed huge growth in the last few years.

13. Using www.londonstockexchange.com, find the current share price for Tesco plc. **(1 mark)**

_____

14. Explain the benefits of Tesco being a plc. **(5 marks)**

_____
_____
_____
_____
_____

Topic 1.2 Understanding the context in which businesses operate

Products such as iPhones, Playstations and designer hats all have to go through the production process, starting with the primary sector and ending in the tertiary sector. All our favourite items have to start as raw materials before they are transformed.

15. Write a primary resource in the first box below. Then complete the secondary and tertiary boxes, showing how the resource could be manufactured to produce a product. **(3 marks)**

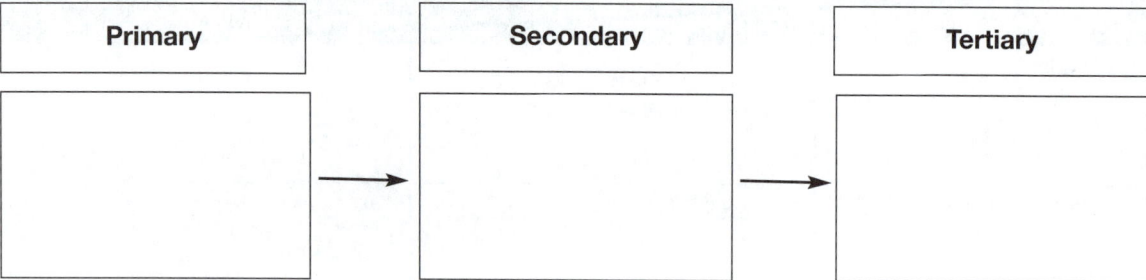

1.2 Understanding the context in which businesses operate

Businesses have to operate in an environment that is affected by legal, economic and political factors and frameworks. The UK government and the European Union have a major influence on the UK business environment, for example, through the way they regulate interest rates and competition. The questions and activities that follow provide you with opportunities to develop and show your understanding of:

- *the role of government*, e.g. European, national, local, growth, full employment, inflation/deflation, surpluses, competitiveness, equality
- *business environment characteristics*, e.g. markets, trends (employment, income, growth), relative growth/decline by sector, decline of primary and secondary industries, growth of tertiary service industries, legal framework.

Questions and activities

On the 24 March 2010, the Chancellor of the Exchequer, Alistair Darling, announced the new budget. He announced an increase in support for small businesses. This will come in the form of financial grants and tax reductions.

1. What are the benefits to the government of its supporting small businesses? **(3 marks)**

_____

_____

_____

Unit 1 Understanding the purpose and ownership of business

James Dyson has become a leading figure in entrepreneurship and innovation. His company, Dyson, has now become the industry's leading producer of vacuum cleaners. It has now even branched into hand dryers!

2. Why is it important that the UK government supports businesses like Dyson? **(4 marks)**

___

Since it started manufacturing in the UK, Toyota has invested nearly £2 billion in its manufacturing plants in Wales and Derbyshire. Toyota now employs over 4,300 people at these plants. The UK government focuses on attracting foreign companies, like Toyota, to start operating from the UK.

3. How could the government encourage companies like Toyota, Honda and IBM to come to the UK? **(4 marks)**

___

Since joining the EU, the UK has been able to increase the number of countries it can trade with.

In 2002, the 'Just dance' show company saw its profits almost double because of links built with EU countries. The expansion in its production was made possible by EU government grants which aim to help smaller businesses expand and accesses other markets.

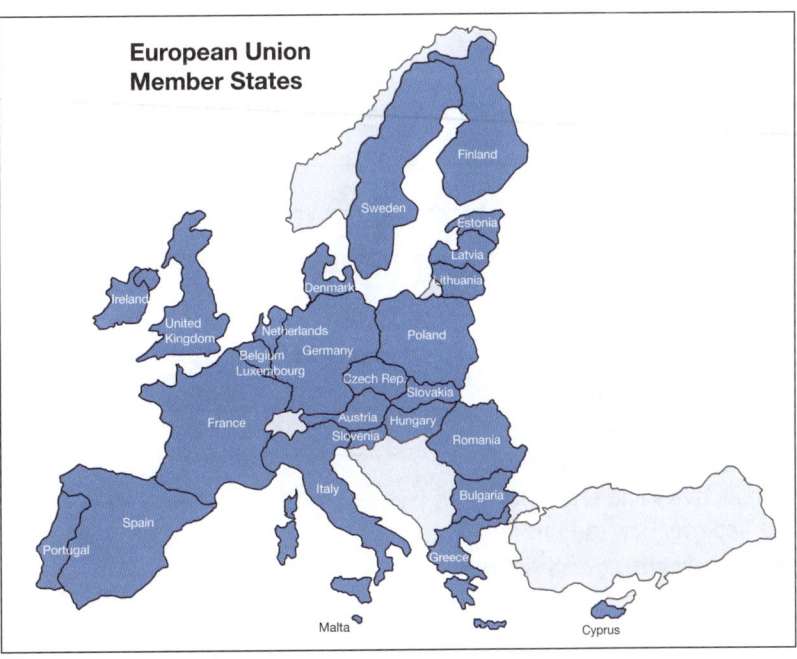

4. How has being part of the EU helped 'Just dance' to increase its profits? **(3 marks)**

___

7

Topic 1.2 Understanding the context in which businesses operate

5. Evaluate the impact on 'Just dance' of the UK leaving the EU, if this were ever to happen. **(8 marks)**

_____
_____
_____
_____
_____
_____
_____
_____

> All different levels of the government have common aims. These are low unemployment and low inflation. Since the UK went into recession, unemployment has risen above the government's target.

6. Define the term 'unemployment'. **(1 mark)**

_____
_____

7. Define the term 'inflation'. **(1 mark)**

_____
_____

8. Why does a government want low unemployment? **(3 marks)**

_____
_____
_____

> Malik Ltd manufactures television sets, which its then sells on to the top brands. The recent rise in unemployment has allowed productivity and efficiency to improve. How can this be?

9. Explain why the availability of employees has benefitted Malik Ltd. **(5 marks)**

_____
_____
_____
_____
_____

10. Explain how rising inflation cold impact Malik Ltd. **(6 marks)**

_____
_____
_____
_____
_____
_____

Unit 2 — Business organisations

This unit covers the following topics:
- business aims and objectives
- the main functional areas in business organisations.

Your learning in this unit will be assessed through assignments that are set and marked by your tutor in accordance with grading criteria and standards set by Edexcel. The assignments will require you to focus on:
- the aims and objectives of different types of business organisation
- the organisational structures and departmental functions of contrasting businesses.

The questions and activities that follow provide you with an opportunity to develop your knowledge and assess your understanding of the range of topics that are part of Unit 2.

Answers can be found at: www.collinseducation.com/btecbusiness

2.1 Setting business aims and objectives

There are a number of different types of business in the United Kingdom. As a result, different types of businesses have a range of differing aims and objectives. The questions and activities that follow provide you with opportunities to develop and show your understanding of:

▶ *aims and objectives*: mission, aims (the long-term visions or goals of a business), objectives (SMART targets – specific, measurable, achievable, realistic, time-constrained – to help achieve the overall aims of a business), purpose of objectives in providing a business focus (e.g. break even, growth, profit maximisation, survival, market share, sales, service provision), relationship with other businesses, failing to meet aims and objectives, business consequences

▶ *sectors*: government, private, public, not-for-profit, voluntary.

Questions and activities

Amazon has grown to be one of the largest online companies in the world. Its aim remains: 'Make history and have fun'. It is a light-hearted aim which has helped them achieve huge success.

Divine Chocolate Ltd has set a more serious aim of 'improving the livelihood of smallholder cocoa producers in West Africa by establishing their own dynamic branded proposition in the UK chocolate market'. Whatever the business, an aim is the first step to success.

1. Define what an 'aim' is in a business context. **(1 mark)**

2. Why is it important that companies like Divine set themselves an aim? **(3 marks)**

3. Discuss whether it is necessary for all companies to set themselves aims, and if so, why. **(6 marks)**

Unit 2 Business organisations

Duke Maintenance was recently set up as a sole trader. Glenn, the owner, is unsure what he should set as his aims and objectives. He works mainly in Croydon and has generated a healthy customer base.

4. Suggest an aim for Duke Maintenance. **(2 marks)**

_____
_____
_____
_____
_____

Different businesses set themselves different aims depending on their size, scale and the industry they are in. Some businesses are purely motivated by profit and growth, whereas others aim to deliver the best service or provide the best goods.

5. In the table below, choose the most appropriate businesses for each aim. Choose from: IKEA, Richer Sounds, Malik Ltd, Save the Children Charity and Dukes Maintenance. **(5 marks)**

Aim	Company
Survival	
Increasing market share	
Growth	
Maximising profit	
Breaking even	

6. What is meant by the term 'objective'? **(1 mark)**

_____

7. What does the acronym SMART stand for? **(5 marks)**

S _____
M _____
A _____
R _____
T _____

11

Topic 2.2 The main functional areas in business organisations

> Save the Children has been fighting for proper healthcare, food, education and protection for all the world's children for over 90 years. Their website shows their mission statement, which reads, 'we deliver immediate and lasting improvement to children's lives worldwide'.

8. Give an example of an aim a not-for-profit organisation may have. **(2 marks)**

   _____
   _____
   _____

9. Why does Save the Children set out a mission statement? **(2 marks)**

   _____
   _____

10. 'Businesses always achieve their aims.' Discuss whether you agree with this statement. **(8 marks)**

    _____
    _____
    _____
    _____
    _____
    _____
    _____
    _____
    _____

2.2 The main functional areas in business organisations

Businesses organise themselves in particular ways in order to achieve their aims and objectives. As businesses grow in size they organise themselves around specialist areas of activity, such as purchasing, sales and stock management. These different areas within a business organisation have to function and link together effectively. The questions and activities that follow provide you with opportunities to develop and show your understanding of:

▶ *functional areas*: sales, production, purchasing, administration, customer service, distribution, finance, human resources, ICT, marketing, research and development (R and D), purposes of functional areas in supporting business aims and objectives, developing new markets, developing new products, using information technology to integrate functional areas

▶ *links*: relationships and interactions with other functional areas, external links (e.g. suppliers, customers, banks, government agencies), information flows, flow of goods and services.

Unit 2 Business organisations

Questions and activities

> Since its launch in January 2007, the iPhone has helped Apple Inc. to achieve record profits. The business has grown into a global leader of technology. The departments have had to adapt, and communication between each functional area has been put under pressure.

1. Give three different functional areas within Apple. **(3 marks)**

   _____
   _____
   _____

2. Explain why the sales team are so important to Apple's continuous success. **(3 marks)**

   _____
   _____
   _____

> Commission is often used as an incentive to motivate staff to work harder. Sales staff are often paid in this way, in the hope that they will be more productive. Some experts believe that this method can actually de-motivate staff and cause sales to drop.

3. What is meant by the term 'commission'? **(2 marks)**

   _____
   _____
   _____

> In 2009, car sales started to plummet. The recession had left new cars a very low priority for many people. Car companies were forced to lower prices, offer low interest rates and move a lot of staff onto commission pay.

4. Explain why commission can cause a drop in motivation. **(4 marks)**

   _____
   _____
   _____
   _____

> Coca Cola has become the world's most recognised brand. Its marketing team continues to work on new ways to bring the company to the forefront of the customer's mind.

5. Describe three duties performed by the marketing department. **(3 marks)**

   _____
   _____
   _____
   _____

13

Topic 2.2 The main functional areas in business organisations

6. List three ways in which the marketing department at Coca Cola promotes its product. **(3 marks)**

> Primeval Productions was set up in 2008 by Edward and his brother James. They both had extensive experience in manufacturing products all over the world. In 2009, they signed a contract with Samsung to produce a revolutionary new phone. To start with, production was going well, until an increase in orders caused problems to occur. Productivity slowed and quality dropped, raising concerns that Primeval Productions wasn't coping.

7. Describe three duties a production employee may perform. **(3 marks)**

8. Suggest two ways in which Primeval Productions could improve the quality of its products. **(2 marks)**

> Edward and James currently employ 24 people at Primeval Productions. They are all semi-skilled workers who have limited experience in production. James has been trying to convince Edward that the only way Primeval Productions is going to improve is by bringing in new machinery which will reduce costs and improve quality.

9. Discuss three advantages the new machinery could bring to Primeval Productions. **(3 marks)**

10. To what extent do you agree with James that the new machinery is the best way to improve quality? **(6 marks)**

Unit 2 Business organisations

> Once the phones have been produced, Edward is responsible for arranging their delivery across Europe. Edward and two other employees form the distribution/logistics department.

11. Describe two key tasks that the logistics department would perform at Primeval Productions. **(2 marks)**

_____
_____
_____
_____

> In 2008, O2 won the best customer service complaints award. Each year O2 invests huge amounts of money to train and improve its staff. In the phone market, companies rely on their customer service team to keep customers happy at a time when brand loyalty is no longer as important.

12. How does O2 monitor its customer service? **(2 marks)**

_____
_____
_____

13. Why is customer service so important to O2? **(3 marks)**

_____
_____
_____
_____

14. Discuss the implications of poor customer service for a company like O2. **(6 marks)**

_____
_____
_____
_____
_____
_____

> The HR department at Tesco has a huge responsibility to help the company to continue to grow. The pressures of recruiting staff have increased since Tesco started to open more and more stores nationwide. Despite individual superstores being responsible for their own recruitment, Tesco plc head office deals with a variety of staffing issues.

15

Topic 2.2 The main functional areas in business organisations

15. Explain three tasks the HR department at Tesco is responsible for. **(3 marks)**

_____
_____
_____

> Tesco, just like many other supermarkets, has a high staff turnover. This can cause both positive and negative effects on Tesco.

16. Define the term 'staff turnover'. **(2 marks)**

_____
_____
_____

17. Discuss the impact of a high staff turnover for Tesco. **(6 marks)**

_____
_____
_____
_____
_____
_____

> There are also other functional areas within a business, such as ICT, Research and Development, Finance and Administration. All these departments play an integral part in any business. The larger the business, the more important communication becomes between these areas. As Nike has become a global brand, recognised by millions of people worldwide, the functional areas within the organisation have had to work together in new ways.

18. Explain how the following functional areas of Nike work together:

Marketing and Finance **(2 marks)**

_____
_____

HR and ICT **(2 marks)**

_____
_____

Production and Sales **(2 marks)**

_____
_____

Unit 3: Financial forecasting for business

This unit covers the following topics:
- costs, profits and revenues
- break-even analysis
- cash flow forecasts.

Your learning in this unit will be assessed through assignments that are set and marked by your tutor in accordance with grading criteria and standards set by Edexcel. The assignments will require you to focus on:
- costs, revenues and profits in a business organisation
- break-even analysis
- cash flow forecasting.

The questions and activities that follow provide you with an opportunity to develop your knowledge and assess your understanding of the range of topics that are part of Unit 3.

Answers can be found at: www.collinseducation.com/btecbusiness

3.1 Costs, revenues and profits in a business organisation

The management and flow of money is at the heart of business activity. Businesses seek to generate revenue (income) but also have to pay a number of different types of costs (expenses) through their everyday trading activities. All businesses have costs. Whether the business is a plc like Marks and Spencer, publicly owned like the NHS or a small enterprise run by a sole trader, they all have similar costs.

The questions and activities that follow provide you with opportunities to develop and show your understanding of:

- *start-up costs*: those the business pays when first setting up
- *running costs*: those the business has to pay on a day-to-day basis
- *fixed costs*: those that do not change in relation to sales or production output (e.g. rent)
- *variable costs*: those that do change in relation to sales/output (e.g. raw materials)
- *revenue*: sources of revenue, e.g. sales, leasing interest, calculating total revenue (unit sales price x number of units sold)
- *calculating gross and net profit*: revenue (income) minus costs (expenditure), cost of sales, expenses (operating costs), maximising profits (increasing revenue).

Questions and activities

> Ramin has always been interested in fashion and has seen a gap for a men's clothing shop in his home town. The town has a number of independent boutiques catering for women, but nothing for men. He has found an empty shop that was once a pet store and now has to start identifying the equipment he needs to make the shop suitable for his venture.

1. Complete the table below, showing which costs are start-up costs and which are running costs. Choose 12 from: decoration, rent, rates, electricity, changing room curtains, sofa, till, counter, rails, stock, wages, signage, light fittings, advertising, water rates, bags for purchases **(12 marks)**

Start-up costs	Running costs

Unit 3 Financial forecasting for business

2. Ramin has to see his bank manager to arrange a business loan. The bank manager has asked him to explain what fixed costs are and what he thinks his will be. Write the answers for Ramin below. **(4 marks)**

___

3. The bank manager also wants Ramin to explain what variable costs are and what he anticipates his will be. Write the answers for Ramin below. **(4 marks)**

___

4. All businesses need revenue to cover their costs. What is the formula for calculating revenue? **(1 mark)**

___

> Ramin has now opened his store 'Homme' and is trying to calculate his profits.

5. Explain, with a formula, what gross profit is. **(4 marks)**

___

6. Explain, with a formula, what net profit is. **(4 marks)**

___

7. Ramin has calculated that his average weekly sales level is £2,200, and to achieve this he spends £800 on stock. Calculate his gross profit. **(2 marks)**

___

8. Ramin's weekly running costs (not including stock) are £1,000. Calculate his net profit. **(2 marks)**

___

19

Topic 3.2 Break-even analysis

9. If Ramin is able to source his products from a cheaper supplier, calculate his gross profit, where his weekly sales level remains at £2,200 and his stock costs £625. **(2 marks)**

10. Ramin has also managed to lower his expenses to £890. Calculate his net profit. **(2 marks)**

3.2 Break-even analysis

Businesses generally try to make a profit. For this to happen, revenues (income) must exceed costs (expenditure). All businesses need to know their break-even point, where revenues equal costs – until this point the will be making a loss, but after it they will be making a profit. The questions and activities that follow provide you with opportunities to develop and show your understanding of:

▶ *break even*: balancing costs or expenditure with revenues or income, areas of profit and loss, margin of safety, methods of presenting graphically.

Questions and activities

1. What is the formula to calculate a business's break-even point? **(1 mark)**

Kate runs an organic grocers in her home town of Minehead in Somerset. She has been established for 3 years and is very successful. A number of her customers have asked her to start selling homemade cakes. Kate is investigating introducing a luxury range of organic cakes.

The cost of the cakes has been estimated as follows:

Fixed costs per month	£800
Variable costs	£1.20 per cake

Each cake is expected to sell for £2.99.

The maximum sales per month are 2,000 cakes.

Unit 3 Financial forecasting for business

2. Use the data on page 20 to construct a fully labelled break-even chart on the graph paper below. Label the break-even point. **(12 marks)**

   You may find it useful to complete this table before constructing the chart.

Number of cakes sold	0	1,000	2,000
Fixed costs			
Variable costs			
Total costs			
Total revenue			

Break-even chart for Kate's organic cakes

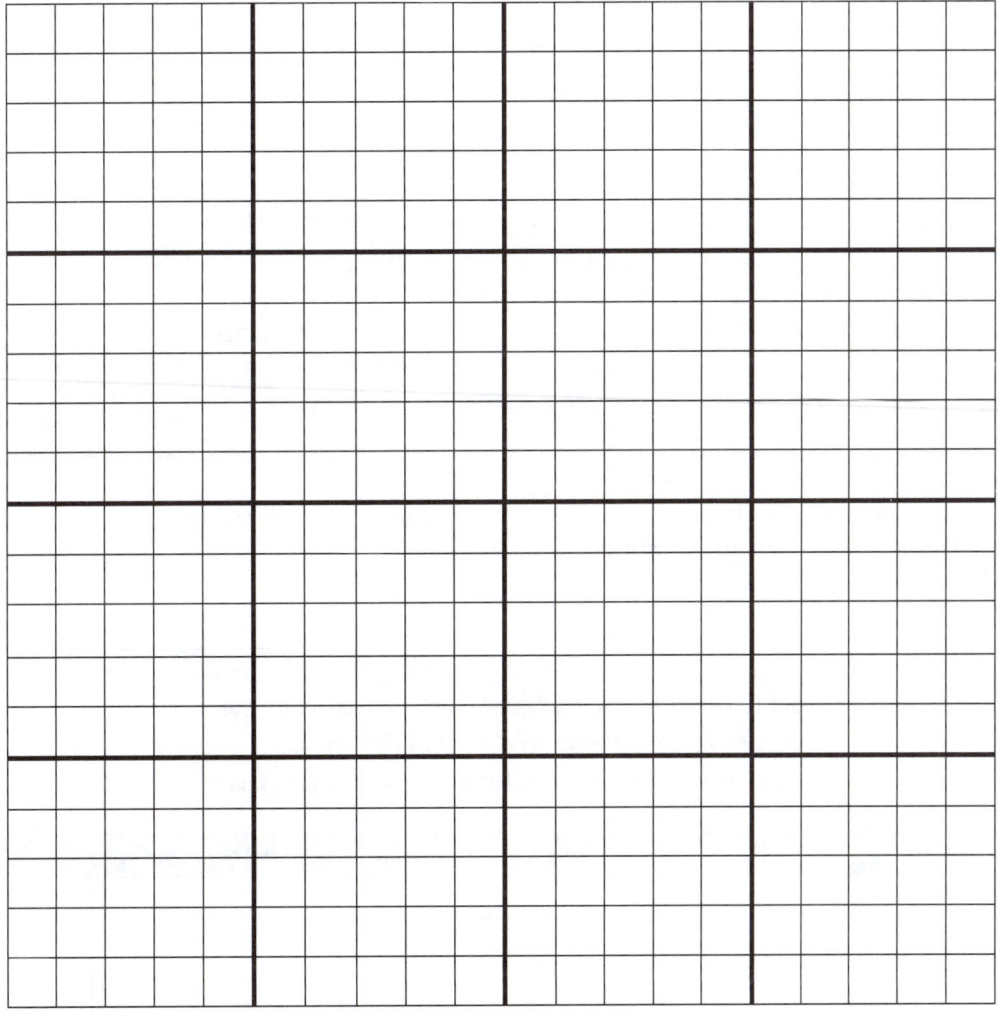

3. Explain what is meant by 'margin of safety'. **(2 marks)**

   _____
   _____

21

Topic 3.2 Break-even analysis

4. Label the margin of safety on the graph you drew for Kate's organic cakes. **(2 marks)**

5. Check that your graph is correct by using the break-even formula to calculate Kate's break-even point. **(2 marks)**

6. Based on your calculations, explain whether you think Kate should launch her range of luxury organic cakes. **(2 marks)**

Helen and David Madueno-Jones run a small country hotel in Andalucia. They have recently arranged a wedding for an English couple and are now looking at introducing a wedding package for English tourists in an effort to increase revenue and make better use of the function room they have on the premises.

The costs of each wedding have been estimated as follows:

Fixed costs per year	£16,000
Variable costs	£1,950 per wedding

Each wedding package for 12 guests staying for 2 nights' full board is £4,500

The maximum sales per year are 50.

7. Using the break-even formula, calculate the break-even point for Helen and David's wedding package. **(2 marks)**

8. Use the data above to construct a fully labelled break-even chart on the graph paper on page 23. Label the break-even point. **(12 marks)**

You may find it useful to complete this table before constructing the chart.

Number of wedding packages sold	0	25	50
Fixed costs			
Variable costs			
Total costs			
Total revenue			

Break-even chart for the Spanish wedding package

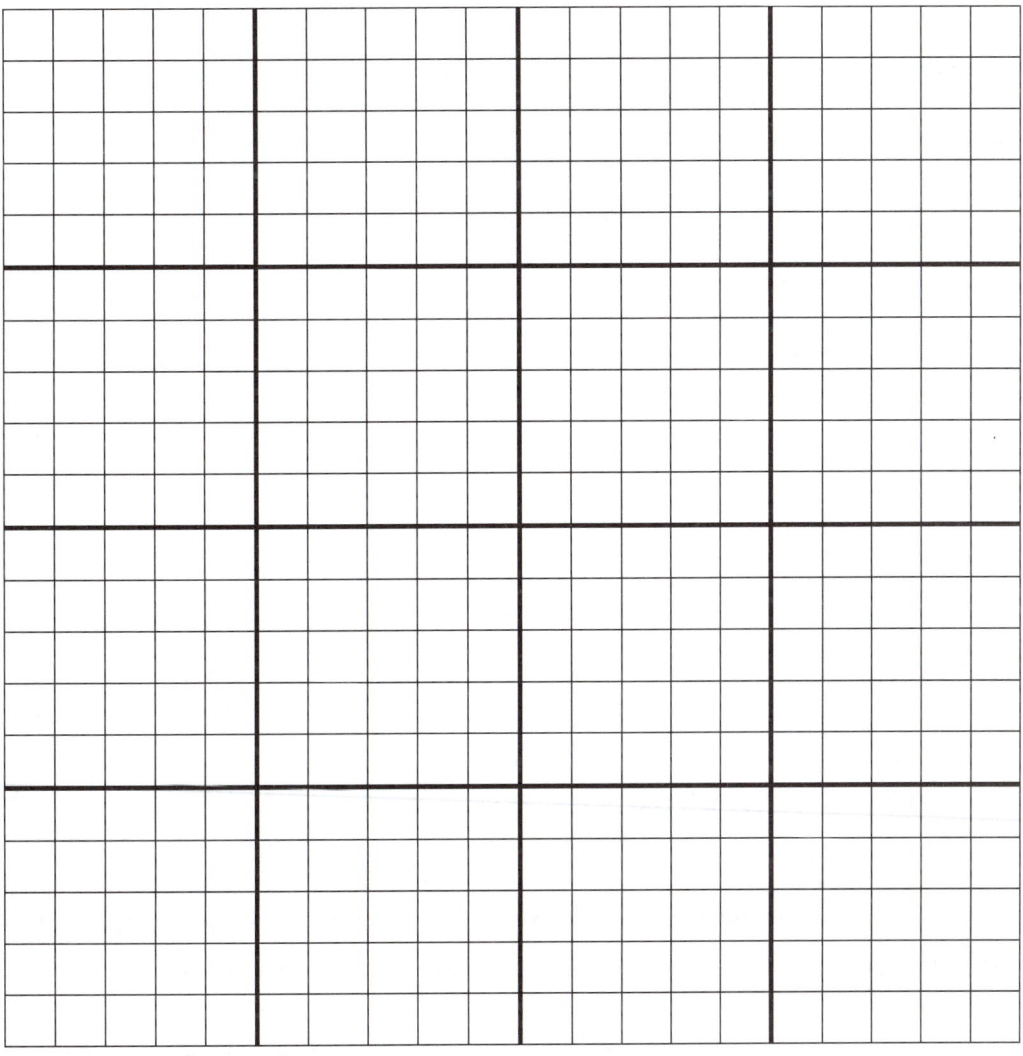

9. Based on your calculations, explain whether you think Helen and David should launch their wedding packages. **(2 marks)**

_____
_____

10. What is the margin of safety for the wedding packages? **(2 marks)**

_____
_____

3.3 Creating a cash flow forecast

Financial management and control are important aspects of business activity. Businesses need to be able to predict or forecast the inflows and outflows of cash into the business over a specified period. To do this, cash flow forecasts are created to enable the business to make decisions about when they need to borrow money, make payments and invest revenues. The questions and activities that follow provide you with opportunities to develop and show your understanding of:

- *cash flow*: capital, sales, loans, regular and irregular inflows, timing of inflows
- *cash outflows*: purchases, loan repayments, wages, regular and irregular outflows, timing of outflows
- *cash balances*: opening balance, closing balance, income per period, expenditure per period.

Questions and activities

Russell Brenton has retired as a plumber and plans to start his own plumbing business called TAPS (The All Round Plumbing Service). He will start his business with savings of £5,000.

In January he plans to purchase a van for £4,500.

He is to lease a workshop at a rent of £600 per month.

He expects his sales to be £3,000 per month.

He plans to spend £250 per month on advertising.

His van should cost around £300 a month to run.

His purchases will cost around £700 per month.

His overheads should be £250 per month.

He plans to pay himself £1,200 a month

1. Identify the cash inflows and cash outflows for Russell. Complete the table below using the information above. **(8 marks)**

Inflows	Outflows

2. Produce a cash flow forecast for TAPS. **(15 marks)**

	Jan	Feb	March	April	TOTAL
OPENING BALANCE AT BANK					
RECEIPTS					
TOTAL					
PAYMENTS					
TOTAL					
NET CASH FLOW					
CLOSING BANK BALANCE					

3. Based on your forecast, in which months should Russell arrange a bank overdraft? **(2 marks)**

_____

_____

Topic 3.3 Creating a cash flow forecast

4. Complete a forecast for Russell for the next 4 months based on the information you have. **(12 marks)**

	May	June	July	August	TOTAL
OPENING BALANCE AT BANK					
RECEIPTS					
TOTAL					
PAYMENTS					
TOTAL					
NET CASH FLOW					
CLOSING BANK BALANCE					

5. Based on your cash flow forecast, would you advise Russell to start this business venture? Explain your answer. **(4 marks)**

_____
_____
_____
_____

Unit 3 Financial forecasting for business

On 1 January Farrah Abassy will start her courier service with £7,000 capital.

She will buy a motorbike in January for £1,500.

She will employ an administrative assistant at a cost of £900 per month.

She will rent a small office for £300 per month.

Her sales should be £2,000 per month from January to March and £3,100 April to June. She is giving all her customers one month's credit.

Her expenses should be £450 per month, rising to £650 from May.

She will pay herself £1,500 a month

6. Produce a 6-month cash flow forecast for Farrah Abassy. **(12 marks)**

	Jan	Feb	March	April	May	June	TOTAL
OPENING BALANCE AT BANK							
RECEIPTS							
TOTAL							
PAYMENTS							
TOTAL							
NET CASH FLOW							
CLOSING BANK BALANCE							

Topic 3.3 Creating a cash flow forecast

7. Farrah has offered all her customers one month's credit. Why would she have offered them this facility? **(2 marks)**

8. What problems has offering this facility to her customers caused Farrah? **(2 marks)**

9. How would you suggest that Farrah overcomes these problems? Analyse the possible impacts of your suggestions on the business. **(6 marks)**

10. A forecast is a prediction and, as we all know from weather forecasts, predictions are not always accurate. Why do you think the bank will want to see a small business person's cash flow forecast before agreeing to give them a business loan? **(6 marks)**

Unit 4: People in organisations

This unit covers the following topics:
- job roles and their functions in organisations
- documentation specific to job roles
- preparation for employment and planning career development.

Your learning in this unit will be assessed through assignments that are set and marked by your tutor in accordance with grading criteria and standards set by Edexcel. The assignments will require you to focus on:
- investigating job roles, functions and structures
- producing documentation for job roles and recruitment
- assessing your readiness for employment and creating career development plans.

The questions and activities that follow provide you with an opportunity to develop your knowledge and assess your understanding of the range of topics that are part of Unit 4.

Answers can be found at: www.collinseducation.com/btecbusiness

Topic 4.1 Job roles and functions in organisations

4.1 Job roles and functions in organisations

Businesses depend on the people they employ. Recruiting high-calibre people who are able to perform specific job roles effectively is a key part of business activity. Every business organisation has to fill a number of different types of job role. The questions and activities that follow provide you with opportunities to develop and show your understanding of:

▶ *job roles and functions*: directors (e.g. looking after interests of shareholders, deciding policy or strategy), managers (e.g. motivating staff, target setting, recruitment and dismissal, allocating work, communicating, planning, decision-making, problem-solving), supervisors/team leaders (e.g. managing operatives, motivating, allocating tasks), operatives (e.g. day-to-day general work), assistants or support staff (e.g. clerical duties)

▶ *organisational structures*, e.g. hierarchal, flat, matrix, functional, divisional.

Questions and activities

E-Studies Ltd designs and develops new interactive resources for GCSE subjects such as Business Studies, Geography and History. The business, started in 2003, has grown year on year and now employs over 40 staff. Andre, the Director, has recently hired a new manager, Steven, to help with the continuous expansion and day-to-day running of the company.

1. Outline three duties the director, Andre, will carry out. **(2 marks)**

_____
_____

Steven has to recruit some new designers to produce up-to-date resources. The recruitment process is just one of the responsibilities Steven has at E-Studies Ltd.

2. Describe three other responsibilities Steven will have at E-Studies Ltd. **(3 marks)**

_____
_____
_____

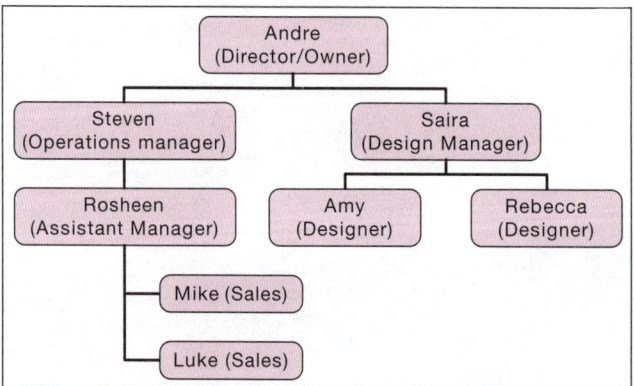

Organisation chart for E-Studies Ltd

30

Unit 4 People in organisations

3. The diagram on page 30 shows the organisation chart for E-Studies Ltd. Is the structure hierarchical or flat? **(1 mark)**

___

> Amy is a new designer recently employed by E-Studies Ltd. She wishes to give Andre an idea for a new product which she thinks will make the company a lot of money!

4. Using the organisational chart on page 30, explain how the idea will travel from Amy to Andre. **(3 marks)**

___

5. Discuss whether a hierarchical structure is better than a flat structure for E-Studies Ltd. **(8 marks)**

> As companies grow, communication between staff becomes more and more difficult. Passing instructions from the Board of Directors to the part-time weekend staff can be a tough test for a thriving business. Since 1997, Divine Chocolate has grown into a global producer of Fairtrade chocolate bars. The company is unique, as the Kuapa Kokoo farmers in Ghana make the key decisions. This can make communication very difficult.

6. Why is communication vital for a business to succeed? **(2 marks)**

___

7. Why does the structure of Divine Chocolate make good communication so important? **(4 marks)**

___

> Evolve Homes began trading in 1999. Since then the business has built over 12,000 new homes all over the UK. The owner, Joseph, has installed a functional structure with departments for accounts, design, management and marketing.

8. What is meant by 'functional structure'? **(2 marks)**

___

9. There are six layers in Evolve Homes' organisational structure. Would this be tall or flat? **(1 mark)**

___

31

10. 'The organisational structure is definitely the best one for us,' said Joseph. Do you agree with this statement? **(8 marks)**

_____
_____
_____
_____
_____
_____
_____
_____
_____
_____

4.2 Producing documentation for specific job roles

Business organisations produce job descriptions and person specifications to ensure that they recruit the best people for specific job roles. The questions and activities that follow provide you with opportunities to develop and show your understanding of:

- *methods of drawing up a job description and a person specification*: department (e.g. staff in the department draw up a description of what the job entails and the qualities required), existing job holder (e.g. current job holder draws up a description and lists the qualities required), interview (e.g. current job holder is interviewed to find out what is involved and the qualities required of the new recruit)
- *contents of a job description*: title, location, description of organisation's business, purpose of job, main tasks, standards required, pay and benefits, promotion prospects, lines of reporting
- *contents of a person specification*: attainments (e.g. qualifications), special aptitudes (e.g. numeracy), interests, personal qualities/disposition (e.g. leadership qualities), circumstances (e.g. mobile or not), competency profiles (e.g. what the candidate should be able to do)
- *applying for jobs*: job specifications, person specifications, application forms, curriculum vitae, letters of application, preparing for interviews (e.g. preparation, dress, research, questions to ask, question anticipation, confidence, body language, voice).

Unit 4 People in organisations

Questions and activities

> Edward has just left university and is now on the job hunt! He has achieved a 2.1 in Business Management and feels he will be ideally suited to a job in the city. Having spoken to his university tutor, Edward feels he has all the attributes and skills to be a successful businessman.
>
> After reading the job description, Edward decides to apply for a job at HSBC bank, situated in Canary Wharf.

1. What is a job description? **(2 marks)**

   _____

   _____

2. Why is it important that Edward reads this document? **(3 marks)**

   _____

   _____

   _____

3. HSBC always provides a job description for every vacancy it advertises. What are the benefits to HSBC of doing this? **(4 marks)**

   _____

   _____

   _____

   _____

> Below is a job description for a job at E-Studies Ltd:
>
> **Marketing Director**
>
> E-Studies Ltd was set up in 2003 and now employs over 40 full-time staff. The business continues to develop a range of interactive and up-to-date resources for all subjects at GCSE level. The company aims to 'revolutionise revision'.
>
> The vacancy will allow a suitably qualified candidate the opportunity to develop the reputation of this growing company and help to improve its national image. The role has become available due to internal promotion. There is plenty of potential for internal promotion within the organisation.
>
> The ideal candidate will have excellent grades in both GCSE and BTEC (or equivalent) and have graduated from university with a good honours degree (2.1 or better). We would expect the candidate to be able to show experience in marketing, with a proven track record of success. The role requires someone with excellent management and organisational skills.
>
> The successful candidate will receive £35,000–£45,000 (depending on experience).
>
> You will report on a weekly basis to the Director of the company.

4. List three elements that are missing from the job description above. **(3 marks)**

   _____

   _____

   _____

33

Topic 4.2 Producing documentation for specific job roles

5. Would you advise Edward to apply for this job? Explain your answer.
   (6 marks)

_____
_____
_____
_____
_____
_____
_____
_____

Once the job description has been written, a person specification is also needed. This will include details of any skills that are essential and any skills that are desirable.

6. Manchester United has advertised for a new club physiotherapist due to the growing injury list.

   Decide whether the skills and qualifications in the table below should be described as essential or desirable in the job specification. **(5 marks)**

Skill or qualification	Essential or desirable?
Driving licence	
Physiotherapist degree	
Ability to work as part of a team	
Available to work weekends	
A sense of humour	

A CV is a vital document when applying for a job. The layout of a CV and the impression it gives are crucial, as a good CV can put one applicant above others in the eyes of the employer.

7. In which part of your CV would you put the points below? **(5 marks)**

Topic	Part of the CV
Like to play rugby.	
Two weeks' work experience at Volkswagen.	
Educated at John Fisher school, Sutton.	
I want to be a world-class reporter.	
British	

After spending hours reading, researching and writing, Maria was ready to send off her application form, CV and covering letter to Virgin Racing.

After a few days, Maria received a phone call inviting her to interview. She was excited, obviously, but suddenly became very worried she would not make a good impression.

8. Suggest three things Maria should do before the interview. **(3 marks)**

_____
_____
_____

Having arrived at the interview 10 minutes late, Maria walked in still clipping her hair back. She had forgotten the name of the person she was to ask for at reception. Eventually, she was shown to the boardroom where she was to have her interview. She sat down to begin the interview and, after a few minutes, took out her chewing gum and placed it in the bin.

The interview continued for over an hour and, by the end of it, Maria was wishing she had been more organised.

She received a call later in the day informing her that she hadn't got the job.

9. Identify four mistakes Maria made at her interview. **(4 marks)**

_____
_____
_____
_____

Three weeks later, Maria was finally offered a job working for Mercedes. They sent her a contract of employment through in the post. All she had to do was sign it and the job was secure.

10. What is a contract of employment? **(2 marks)**

_____
_____
_____

4.3 Preparing for employment

Obtaining a job in a business organisation requires careful planning and preparation and the ability to perform well at interview. Progression within an organisation or business sector generally is best achieved by making and working through a career development plan. The questions and activities that follow provide you with opportunities to develop and show your understanding of:

- *personal audit*: knowledge, skills (e.g. technical, practical, communication), matching knowledge and skills to job opportunities
- *types of employment*, e.g. full time, part time, permanent, temporary, seasonal, paid, voluntary

Topic 4.3 Preparing for employment

- *sources of information and advice*: sources (e.g. advertisements, word of mouth, employment/government agencies), advice (e.g. government agencies, careers advisers, tutors, existing and previous employers, careers fairs, friends and family)
- *career development*: in the workplace (e.g. induction, training needs, development plans, performance targets, certificated training, uncertificated training, personal development, flexible working, progression opportunities), in education (e.g. qualifications needed for course entry, length of courses, practical experience entry requirements, progression from education courses to professional training).

Questions and activities

> Every Christmas, department stores like Debenhams, House of Frasier and Alders employ thousands of temporary staff to help meet the huge demand.

1. What type of employment is described above? **(1 marks)**

2. Why is this type of flexible employment beneficial to businesses like these? **(2 marks)**

> Qasim is on the verge of leaving school and feels under pressure to make decisions about his future. Should he go to university? Or should he try to get a well-paid job?

3. Name two different sources of information Qasim can go to for advice. **(2 marks)**

> On his first day working at ExCel Arena, Darren was given thorough induction training. This was very important as he would be in charge of running events for thousands of people, using a range of equipment and staff to help.

4. What is meant by 'induction training'? **(2 marks)**

Unit 4 People in organisations

5. Why is it important that all new employees received induction training? **(4 marks)**

_____
_____
_____
_____

> Six months later, Darren discussed his progress with his manager. He was adamant he had learnt a lot from his role, but he had no qualifications to prove it. In essence, he had not been on any courses to receive any certified training.

6. Explain why a lack of certified training could have a negative effect on Darren's career. **(3 marks)**

_____
_____
_____
_____

7. Why is it important that Darren takes control of his own career? **(5 marks)**

_____
_____
_____
_____
_____
_____

Glossary

Aim: where a business wants to be in the future

Articles of Association: the legal document that shows how the business is to be run

Body language: the impressions given to others by the way a person uses his or her body, to show, for example, boredom, respect, disrespect, anger, sex appeal

Break-even point: this is the sales level at which revenue and costs are equal

Certificate of Incorporation: the legal document showing that a limited liability company has been formed

Commission: income that is dependent on the level of sales an employee makes; usually a percentage of the sales made

Computer hardware: computer equipment that one uses, for example, the hard drive, monitor, keyboard

Cost price: the price charged by a supplier, which is therefore the cost to the purchasing company, for example, a car manufacturer buying tyres from Pirelli

Costs: expenditure; the items on which a business spends its money, such as wages or materials

Covering letter: an important component of applying for a job, this is a brief introduction, which should be sent with a CV; it should include the skills the individual can offer the company and why he or she would be an asset

Curriculum vitae (CV): a document that sets out an individual's skills, achievements and job history

Deed of Partnership: a legally binding agreement between all the partners in a business partnership

Flexible working: jobs that may not be permanent or full time, for example, sharing a job 50/50 with another person

Functional areas: the departments responsible for completing a key operation, for example, finance

Grants: business funding provided by government that does not have to be repaid

Hierarchy: the layers of management within an organisation; it is often drawn as a chart that looks like a pyramid, with the boss on the top

Glossary

Income: the revenue generated by selling items to customers or clients

Inflation: a measurement of the rate of increase in prices throughout an economy

Infrastructure: the basics of modern life such as water, electricity, broadband, motorways and fast rail links

Invoice: the bill issued by a business to a customer, indicating the products, quantities and agreed prices for products and/or services the business has sold to the customer

Job description: a detailed breakdown of what the job consists of

Job function: the tasks involved in the job

Job security: a feeling of confidence that the income received from working at a company will continue for the foreseeable future

Job title: the name given to a particular job role, such as a store manager

Letter of application: similar to a covering letter, but usually longer, as it may not be accompanied by a CV

Limited liability company: all companies have limited liability, i.e. the owners (the shareholders) have control, yet cannot be held responsible personally for any business debts

Margin of safety: the comfort zone between the actual sales and the break-even point

Market share: the percentage of all sales held by one brand or business, for example, a leading chewing gum company has 90% of the UK market, and so has the market share

Memorandum of Association: a legal document that provides details about what a company does and how it has been financed

Mission statement: an aim that is intended to inspire

Multinational: operating in many, or all, countries around the world, such as certain fast food companies and cooldrink manufacturers

Objectives: the specific targets that must be achieved in order to reach the long-term aims

Person specification: the qualifications, experience and qualities required from the job applicant

Personal audit: checking that one's skills and qualifications match the needs of an employer

Private sector: organisations that operate without any government funding, including sole traders, companies and charities

Profit: made when revenues are higher than costs; sales minus the costs paid by the business to make the sale

Glossary

Proof read: thoroughly check a document for accuracy, spelling and consistency

Public sector: organisations financed by government, such as the NHS and state schools

Revenue: this is the value of sales made within a period of time, for example, a year

Sales: the money collected from customers (selling price multiplied by quantity sold)

Shortlist: the names of the job applicants who have passed the initial selection process

Software: computer programs and operating systems such as Microsoft Windows and Microsoft Word

Statutory accounts: the financial information (including a profit and loss account, a balance sheet and a cash flow statement) a company must submit each year to Companies House

Unlimited liability: the business owner is responsible for any and all business debts, and may therefore have to sell personal assets (house, car) to repay these debts

Student notes

Student notes

Student notes

Student notes

Student notes

Student notes

Student notes

Student notes

Student notes

Student notes

Student notes